D'Nealian® Handwriting
Practice and Review Workbook

Letter Instruction

Letter Practice

Everyday Writing

2

Scott Foresman
Addison Wesley

Editorial Offices: Glenview, Illinois
Sales Offices: Reading, Massachusetts • Duluth, Georgia • Glenview, Illinois
Carrollton, Texas • Menlo Park, California

1-800-552-2259
http://www.sf.aw.com

D'Nealian® Handwriting is a registered trademark of Donald Neal Thurber.

ISBN: 0-673-57638-8

8 9 10 11 PO 07 06 05 04

Contents

Getting Started

Writing Posture 4
Letter Sizes 5
Evaluating Handwriting 6–7

Letter and Number Descriptions 8–11

Writing Manuscript Letters

Legibility: Letter Size and Form 12
Legibility: Letter Slant...........................13
Legibility: Letter and Word Spacing.......14
Writing and Practicing **aA** 15–16
Writing and Practicing
   dD and **oO**.........................17–18
Writing and Practicing
   gG and **cC** 19–20
Writing and Practicing
   eE and **sS** 21–22
Review and Evaluation 23–24

Writing and Practicing **fF**.................25–26
Writing and Practicing **bB** and **lL**.....27–28
Writing and Practicing **tT** and **hH** 29–30
Writing and Practicing **kK** 31–32
Review and Evaluation 33–34

Writing and Practicing **il** and **uU**......35–36
Writing and Practicing
   wW and **yY** 37–38
Writing and Practicing **jJ** and **rR** 39–40
Writing and Practicing
   nN and **mM** 41–42
Writing and Practicing **pP** 43–44
Review and Evaluation 45–46

Writing and Practicing
   qQ and **vV**............................47–48
Writing and Practicing **zZ** and **xX** 49–50
Writing and Practicing **1-10** 51–52
Writing and Practicing **one-ten**......53–54
Review and Evaluation 55–56

Writing Cursive Letters

Ready for Cursive..............................57
Strokes That Make Cursive
   Letters.................................58–60
Legibility: Letter Size and Form 61
Legibility: Letter Slant and Spacing.......62
Writing and Practicing **l** and **h** 63–64
Writing and Practicing **k** and **t**........65–66
Writing and Practicing **i** and **u** 67–68
Writing and Practicing **e**.................69–70
Writing and Practicing **j** and **p** 71–72

Review and Evaluation 73–74

Writing and Practicing **a**.................75–76
Writing and Practicing **d** and **c** 77–78
Writing and Practicing **n** and **m** 79–80
Writing and Practicing **g** and **x** 81–82
Writing and Practicing **y** and **q** 83–84
Review and Evaluation 85–86

Writing and Practicing **o** and **w** 87–88
Writing and Practicing **b**.................89–90
Writing and Practicing **v** and **z**........91–92
Writing and Practicing **s** 93–94
Writing and Practicing **r**.................95–96
Writing and Practicing **f**.................97–98
Review and Evaluation 99–100

Legibility: Letter Size and Form 101
Legibility: Letter Slant.......................102
Writing and Practicing
   A and **C**...............................103–104
Writing and Practicing
   E and **O**...............................105–106
Review and Evaluation 107–108

Writing and Practicing
   H and **K** 109–110
Writing and Practicing
   N and **M**...............................111–112
Writing and Practicing
   U and **V**...............................113–114
Writing and Practicing
   Y and **W**...............................115–116
Review and Evaluation 117–118

Writing and Practicing
   T and **F** 119–120
Writing and Practicing **B** 121–122
Writing and Practicing
   P and **R**...............................123–124
Review and Evaluation 125–126

Writing and Practicing
   G and **S**...............................127–128
Writing and Practicing **I**...............129–130
Writing and Practicing
   Z and **Q**...............................131–132
Writing and Practicing **D** 133–134
Writing and Practicing **J** 135–136
Writing and Practicing
   X and **L** 137–138
Review and Evaluation 139–140

Index.................................141

Name _____

Get ready to write.
Sit up tall.
Put your feet on the floor.
Hold your pencil lightly.

Slant your paper.

left-handed

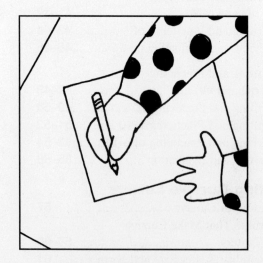

right-handed

4   Children model posture, pencil grip, arm position, and paper position for writing.

Name _____

Use the lines to learn letter size.
Trace these letters.

Write small letters between these lines.

top line

middle line

baseline

descender line

Write tall letters between these lines.

top line

middle line

baseline

descender line

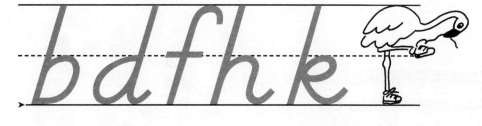

Write letters that fall between these lines.

top line

middle line

baseline

descender line

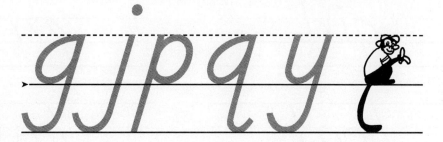

Children review letter sizes.

Name _____

Evaluate Your Handwriting

Check your letters for **size**.
Are your letters written between the correct lines?

Good	Needs Work
boy	*boy*

Check your letters for **shape**.
Are curved lines curved?
Are straight lines straight?
Are closed letters closed?

Good	Needs Work
girl	*girl*
boat	*boat*

Children learn how to evaluate their handwriting.

Name _____

Evaluate Your Handwriting

Check the **slant** of your letters.
Do all of your letters slant the same way?

Good   Needs Work

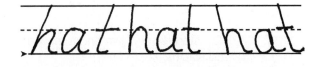

Check your **spacing.**
Are your letters too close together or too far apart?
Are your words too close together or too far apart?

Good   Needs Work

fine   *close   far*

just fine   *tooclose too far*

Children learn how to evaluate their handwriting.

Manuscript Letter Descriptions

Lower-case Letters

a — Middle start; around down, close up, down, and a monkey tail.

b — Top start; slant down, around, up, and a tummy.

c — Start below the middle; curve up, around, down, up, and stop.

d — Middle start; around down, touch, up high, down, and a monkey tail.

e — Start between the middle and bottom; curve up, around, touch, down, up, and stop.

f — Start below the top; curve up, around, and slant down. Cross.

g — Middle start; around down, close up, down under water, and a fishhook.

h — Top start; slant down, up over the hill, and a monkey tail.

i — Middle start; slant down and a monkey tail. Add a dot.

j — Middle start; slant down under water and a fishhook. Add a dot.

k — Top start; slant down, up into a little tummy, and a monkey tail.

l — Top start; slant down and a monkey tail.

m — Middle start; slant down, up over the hill, up over the hill again, and a monkey tail.

n — Middle start; slant down, up over the hill, and a monkey tail.

o — Middle start; around down and close up.

p — Middle start; slant down under water, up, around, and a tummy.

q — Middle start; around down, close up, down under water, and a backward fishhook.

r — Middle start; slant down, up, and a roof.

s — Start below the middle; curve up, around, down, and a snake tail.

t — Top start; slant down and a monkey tail. Cross.

u — Middle start; down, around, up, down, and a monkey tail.

v — Middle start; slant down right and slant up right.

w — Middle start; down, around, up, and down, around, up again.

x — Middle start; slant down right, and a monkey tail. Cross down left.

y — Middle start; down, around, up, down under water, and a fishhook.

z — Middle start; over right, slant down left, and over right.

Capital Letters

A — Top start; slant down left. Same start; slant down right. Middle bar across.

B — Top start; slant down, up, around halfway, close, around again, and close.

C — Start below the top; curve up, around, down, up, and stop.

D — Top start; slant down, up, around, and close.

8

E — Top start; over left, slant down, and over right. Middle bar across.

F — Top start; over left and slant down. Middle bar across.

G — Start below the top, curve up, around, down, up, and over left.

H — Top start; slant down. Another top start, to the right; slant down. Middle bar across.

I — Top start; slant down. Cross the top and the bottom line.

J — Top start; slant down and curve up left.

K — Top start; slant down. Another top start, to the right; slant down left, touch, slant down right, and a monkey tail.

L — Top start; slant down and over right.

M — Top start; slant down. Same start; slant down right halfway, slant up right, and slant down.

N — Top start; slant down. Same start; slant down right, and slant up.

O — Top start; around down and close up.

P — Top start; slant down, up, around halfway, and close.

Q — Top start; around down and close up. Cross with a curve down right.

R — Top start; slant down, up, around halfway, close, slant down right, and a monkey tail.

S — Start below the top; curve up, around, down, and a snake tail.

T — Top start; slant down. Cross the line at the top.

U — Top start; slant down, around, up, down, and a monkey tail.

V — Top start; slant down right and slant up right.

W — Top start; slant down right, slant up right, slant down right, and slant up right again.

X — Top start; slant down right and a monkey tail. Cross down left.

Y — Top start; slant down right halfway. Another top start, to the right; slant down left, and touch on the way.

Z — Top start; over right, slant down left, and over right.

Number Descriptions

1 — Top start; slant down.

2 — Start below the top; curve up, around, and slant down left, and over right.

3 — Start below the top; curve up, around halfway; around again, up, and stop.

4 — Top start; down halfway; over right. Another top start, to the right; slant down and through.

5 — Top start; over left; slant down halfway; curve around, down, up, and stop.

6 — Top start; slant down, and curve around; up, and close.

7 — Top start; over right; slant down left.

8 — Start below the top; curve up, around, down; a snake tail; slant up right; through, and touch.

9 — Top start; curve down, around, close; slant down.

10 — Top start; slant down. Another top start to the right; curve down, around, and close.

Cursive Letter Descriptions

Lower-case Letters

Overhill; back, around down, close up, down, and up.

Uphill high; loop down, around, up, and sidestroke.

Overhill; back, around, down, and up.

Overhill; back, around down, touch, up high, down, and up.

Uphill; loop down, through, and up.

Uphill high; loop down under water, loop up right, touch, and up.

Overhill; back, around down, close up, down under water, loop up left, and through.

Uphill high; loop down, up over the hill, and up.

Uphill; down, and up. Add a dot.

Uphill; down under water, loop up left, and through. Add a dot.

Uphill high; loop down, up into a little tummy, slant down right, and up.

Uphill high; loop down, and up.

Overhill; down, up over the hill, up over the hill again, and up.

Overhill; down, up over the hill, and up.

Overhill; back, around down, close up, and sidestroke.

Uphill; down under water, up, around into a tummy, and up.

Overhill; back, around down, close up, down under water, loop up right, touch, and up.

Uphill; sidestroke, down, and up.

Uphill; down, around, close, and up.

Uphill high; down, and up. Cross.

Uphill; down, around, up, down, and up.

Overhill; down, around, up, and sidestroke.

Uphill; down, around, up, down, around, up again, and sidestroke.

Overhill; slant down right, and up. Cross down left.

Overhill; down, around, up, down under water, loop up left, and through.

Overhill; around down, around again, and down under water, loop up left, and through.

10

Capital Letters

 Top start; around down, close up, down, and up.

 Top start; down, up, around halfway, around again, touch, sidestroke, and stop.

 Start below the top; curve up, around, down, and up.

 Top start; down, loop right, curve up, around, close, loop right, through, and stop.

 Start below the top; curve up, around to the middle, around again to the bottom line, and up.

 Start below the top; down, around, up, and sidestroke. Wavy cross and a straight cross.

 Bottom start; uphill high, loop through the middle, up, curve down, around, through the uphill, sidestroke, and stop.

 Start below the top; make a cane. Top start, to the right; down, up, left, touch, loop right, through, and stop.

 Start below the middle; sidestroke left, curve down, around, uphill high, loop down, and up.

 Bottom start; curve up, around, touch on the way down under water, loop up left, and through.

 Start below the top; make a cane. Top start, to the right; slant down left, touch, slant down right, and up.

 Start below the top; uphill, loop down, loop right, and up.

 Start below the top; make a cane, up over the hill, up over the hill again, and up.

 Start below the top; make a cane, up over the hill, and up.

 Top start; around down, close up, loop right, through, and stop.

 Top start; down, up, around halfway, and close.

 Start below the top; curve up, around, down, loop right, and up.

 Top start; down, up, around halfway, close, slant down right, and up.

 Bottom start; uphill high, loop through the middle, curve down, around, through the uphill, sidestroke, and stop.

 Start below the top; down, around, up, and sidestroke. Wavy cross.

 Start below the top; make a cane, around, up, down, and up.

 Start below the top; make a cane, around, slant up right, sidestroke, and stop.

 Start below the top; make a cane, around, up, down, around, up again, sidestroke, and stop.

 Start below the top; curve up, slant down right, and up. Cross down left.

 Start below the top; make a cane, around up, down under water, loop up left, and through.

 Start below the top; curve up, around, down, around again, and down under water, loop up left, and through.

Name _____

Letter Size and Form

Manuscript letters can be small, tall, or have descenders.

a c e i m n o r s u v w x z

b d f h k l t

g j p q y

Small letters sit on the bottom line. They touch the middle line. Write two small letters.

Tall letters also sit on the bottom line. They touch the top line. Write two tall letters.

Letters with descenders have tails that go down under the bottom line. The descenders touch the line below. Write two letters with descenders.

Handwriting is easy to read when letters are formed correctly. Close letters like **a** and **b**. Cross **t** and **f**. Dot the letters **i** and **j**.

Can you read this word?

gift

Write **gift** correctly. Close the **g**. Dot the **i**. Cross the **f** and the **t**.

The word is **gift**. Why is it hard to read?

© Scott Foresman / Addison Wesley

12

Letter Slant

Slant all your letters and puctuation the same way.
That will make your handwriting easier to read.

Some writers slant their letters to the right.

right

Some writers slant their letters to the left.

left

Some writers make their letters straight up and down.

straight

Do not slant letters different ways.

different

Choose a slant. Then write **Can rabbits be pets?**

_____

_____

Name _____

Letter and Word Spacing

Handwriting is easier to read when letters are evenly spaced.

Don't write letters in a word too close together.

Don't write letters in a word too far apart.

fish

f i s h

Words and punctuation in a sentence also have to be spaced correctly. Leave more space between words than between letters in a word. Trace this sentence. It has correct spacing.

The fish can swim.

Here is a sentence that is not spaced correctly. Do you know what it says? Write the sentence with correct spacing.

C anyoure adthi s?

_____

14

Name _____

Writing Manuscript aA

Trace and write.

a   *a*   *a*

A   *A*   *A*

Amanda   **Aaron**

Amanda   *Aaron*

Anna's parakeet

Anna's parakeet

Letter Descriptions a: Middle start; around down, close up, down, and a monkey tail. **A:** Top start; slant down left. Same start; slant down right. Middle bar across.

Name _____

Practicing Manuscript aA

Trace and write.

Andrea has a rabbit.

Andrea has a rabbit.

Ajax is Ada's cat.

Ajax is Ada's cat.

Alan wants a canary.

Alan wants a canary.

Write about a pet you have or would like to have.

16

Name _____

Writing Manuscript dD and oO

Trace and write.

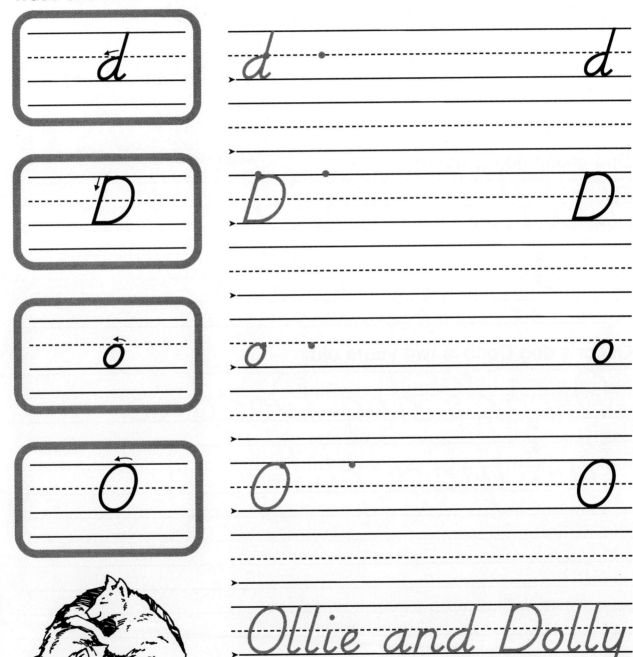

Ollie and Dolly

Letter Descriptions d: Middle start; around down, touch, up high, down, and a monkey tail. **D:** Top start; slant down, up, around, and close. **o:** Middle start; around down, and close up. **O:** Top start; around down, and close up.

© Scott Foresman / Addison Wesley

Name _____

Practicing Manuscript dD and oO

Trace and write.

Dad groomed his horse.

Dad groomed his horse.

Oscar's dog Dodo is two years old.

Oscar's dog Dodo is two years old.

Write the names of two pets you know.

Writing Manuscript gG and cC

Trace and write.

g

G

c

C

Goggles

cucumber

Letter Descriptions g: Middle start; around down, close up, down under water, and a fishhook. G: Start below the top; curve up, around, down, up, and over left. c: Start below the middle; curve up, around, down, up, and stop. C: Start below the top; curve up, around, down, up, and stop.

Practicing Manuscript gG and cC

Trace and write.

Craig

Craig

Cecil

Cecil

Grace

Grace

Goggles the dog ate a gigantic cucumber.

Goggles the dog ate a gigantic cucumber.

Unscramble this sentence.
cabbage crunchy Greg his gerbil gave.

Name _____

Writing Manuscript eE and sS

Trace and write.

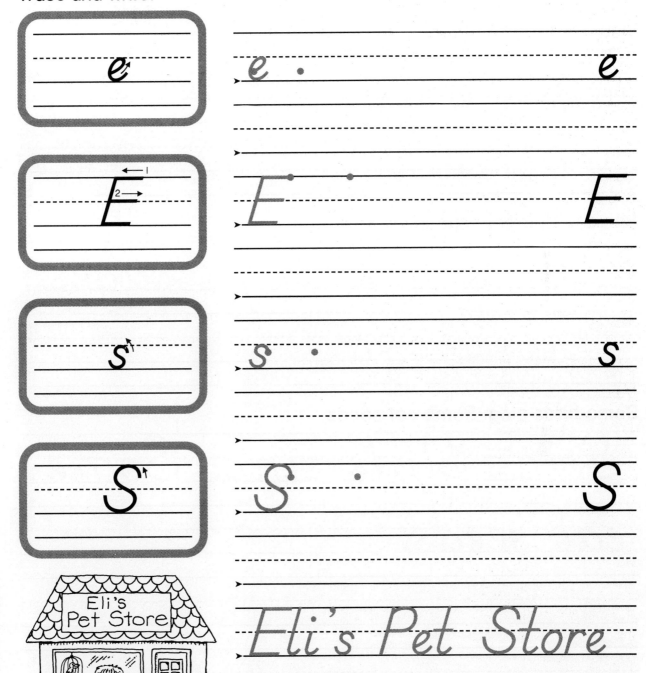

Eli's Pet Store

Letter Descriptions **e:** Start between the middle and bottom; curve up, around, touch, down, up, and stop.
E: Top start; over left, slant down, and over right. Middle bar across. **s:** Start below the middle; curve up, around,
down, and a snake tail. **S:** Start below the top; curve up, around, down, and a snake tail.

Name _____

Practicing Manuscript eE and sS

Trace and write.

Elsa goes to the pet shop.

Elsa goes to the pet shop.

She sees birds in cages.

She sees birds in cages.

Some birds sing. Some eat seeds.

Some birds sing. Some eat seeds.

Name _____

Review

Write the words.

a sad dog _____   **good deeds** _____

_____   _____

➤ _____   ➤ _____

_____   _____

goose eggs _____   **odd cages** _____

_____   _____

➤ _____   ➤ _____

_____   _____

Read the story. Then answer the questions.

Coco was a sad, lost dog. Essie Sue found Coco and took her to Doc Owen, the vet. Doc Owen put an ad in the paper. Ada Gace read the ad and smiled. She was happy someone had found her dog.

Who was lost? _____   **Who owned the dog?** _____

_____   _____

➤ _____   ➤ _____

Who put an ad in the paper? _____   **Who found the dog?** _____

_____   _____

➤ _____   ➤ _____

Name _____

Evaluation

Write the sentences.

Remember: The letters **a**, **d**, **o**, and **g** should be closed. Also, your letters should all slant the same way.

Ginger is a good dog.

Ed and Seth have cats.

Did Angela name her mouse Otto or Coco?

✓ **Check Your Handwriting**   Yes   No
   Are the letters **a**, **d**, **o**, and **g** closed?   ☐   ☐
   Do all your letters slant the same way?   ☐   ☐

24

Writing Manuscript fF

Trace and write.

f

f   *f*   *f*

F

F   *F*

fluffy

fluffy

fifteen

fifteen

Felix and Fran

Felix and Fran

Letter Descriptions f: Start below the top; curve up, around, and slant down. Cross. **F:** Top start; over left, and slant down. Middle bar across.

Practicing Manuscript fF

Trace and write.

Frank and his friends rode for four hours.

Frank and his friends

rode for four hours.

Faye rode fastest of all.

Faye rode fastest of all.

Fritz fell off his bike.

Fritz fell off his bike.

Writing Manuscript bB and lL

Trace and write.

b   b   b

B   B   B

l   l   l

L   L   L

Babs Lubler

Letter Descriptions b: Top start; slant down, around, up, and a tummy. **B:** Top start; slant down, up, around halfway, close, around again, and close. **l:** Top start; slant down, and a monkey tail. **L:** Top start; slant down, and over right.

Practicing Manuscript bB and lL

Trace and write.

Barb

Barb

Bill

Bill

Libby

Libby

Bob's bicycle has a bell.

Bob's bicycle has a bell.

Lilly has a little bike.

Lilly has a little bike.

What's in the box? Write a sentence.

Name _____

Writing Manuscript tT and hH

Trace and write.

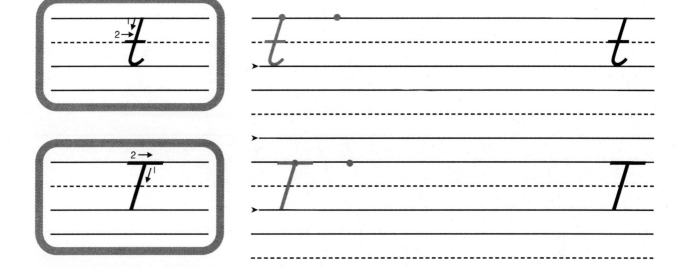

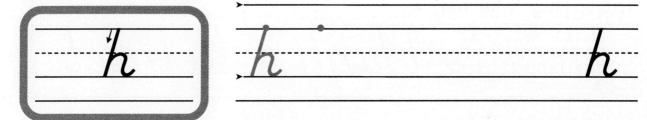

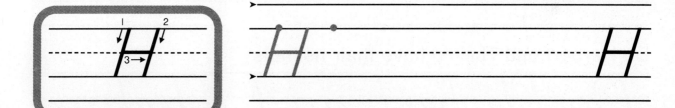

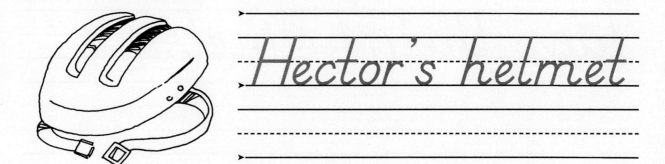

Hector's helmet

Letter Descriptions **t:** Top start; slant down, and a monkey tail. Cross. **T:** Top start; slant down. Cross the top.
h: Top start; slant down, up over the hill, and a monkey tail. **H:** Top start; slant down. Another top start, to the
right; slant down. Middle bar across.

Name _____

Practicing Manuscript tT and hH

Trace and write.

Turn here, Heather.

Turn here, Heather.

This is Hugh's helmet.

This is Hugh's helmet.

Do Herbert and Thelma have their helmets?

Do Herbert and Thelma have their helmets?

Writing Manuscript kK

Trace and write.

k   k   k

K   K   K

kickstand

kickstand

check

check

Kirk

Kirk

Letter Descriptions k: Top start; slant down, up into a little tummy, and a monkey tail. **K:** Top start; slant down. Another top start, to the right; slant down left, touch, slant down right, and a monkey tail.

Name _____

Practicing Manuscript kK

Trace and write.

Keep a bike lock.

Keep a bike lock.

Check your brakes.

Check your brakes.

Pack a backpack.

Pack a backpack.

Write the sentence below in the box. Write smaller
than usual to fit the space.

Kickstands keep bikes standing.

Name _____

Review

Label the bike. Use the words in the box.
Remember to write smaller to fit the space.

front wheel	back wheel	seat
handlebars	kickstand	brakes

Write the names of the riders.

Billie Thatcher   **Kathy Lubbock**   **Frank Hoffberg**

Name _____

Evaluation

Write the sentences.

Remember: The letters **f** and **t** should be crossed. Also, write smaller when you write in a small space.

The Koto family went for a bike ride.

>
>

Bad luck! Flat tires!

>

Luckily, Hal saw a sign.

>

Write this sentence on the sign.
**This way to Hank's
Bike-Fix-It Shop.**

✓ **Check Your Handwriting**   **Yes**   **No**

Did you cross the letters **f** and **t**?   ☐   ☐

Does your handwriting fit the space?   ☐   ☐

34

Name _____

Writing Manuscript iI and uU

Trace and write.

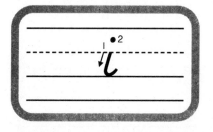 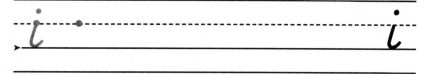

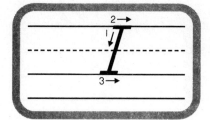 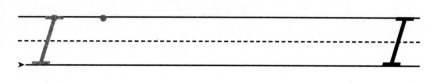

 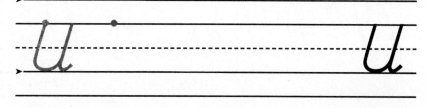

Ida the unicorn

Ida the unicorn

Letter Descriptions i: Middle start; slant down, and a monkey tail. Add a dot. I: Top start; slant down. Cross the top and the bottom line. u: Middle start; down, around, up, down, and a monkey tail. U: Top start; down, around, up, down, and a monkey tail.

Practicing Manuscript iI and uU

Trace and write.

Invite your family and friends to our show.

Invite your family and

friends to our show.

I'll usher in the guests.

I'll usher in the guests.

Up goes the curtain!

Up goes the curtain!

Name _____

Writing Manuscript wW and yY

Trace and write.

w

W

y

y

Yolanda

Yolanda

Letter Descriptions w: Middle start; down, around, up, and down, around, up again. **W:** Top start; slant down right, slant up right, slant down right, and slant up right again. **y:** Middle start; down, around, up, down under water, and a fishhook. **Y:** Top start; slant down right halfway. Another top start, to the right; slant down left, and touch on the way.

Name _____

Practicing Manuscript wW and yY

Trace and write.

Yesterday I worked with Yoshi.

Yesterday I worked

with Yoshi.

We were very busy.

We were very busy.

Wow, what scenery!

Wow, what scenery!

Name _____

Writing Manuscript jJ and rR

Trace and write.

Jeff Roberts

> *Jeff Roberts*

Letter Descriptions **j:** Middle start; slant down under water, and a fishhook. Add a dot. **J:** Top start; slant down, and curve up left. **r:** Middle start; slant down, up, and a roof. **R:** Top start; slant down, up, around halfway, close, slant down right, and a monkey tail.

Name _____

Practicing Manuscript jJ and rR

Trace and write.

Jerry tells great jokes.

Jerry tells great jokes.

Rosa juggles red balls.

Rosa juggles red balls.

Juggling is hard.

Juggling is hard.

Write what you would do at a talent show.

Name _____

Writing Manuscript nN and mM

Trace and write.

n   n   n

N   N   N

m   m   m

M   M   M

Norm and Mei

Norm and Mei

Letter Descriptions n: Middle start; slant down, up over the hill, and a monkey tail. **N:** Top start; slant down. Same start; slant down right, and slant up. **m:** Middle start; slant down, up over the hill, up over the hill again, and a monkey tail. **M:** Top start; slant down. Same start; slant down right halfway, slant up right, and slant down.

Practicing Manuscript nN and mM

Trace and write.

Nick made nine nice animal masks.

Nick made nine nice animal masks.

Mindy needs makeup.

Mindy needs makeup.

Unscramble this sentence.
mended costume Monica's Nina.

Writing Manuscript pP

Trace and write.

p   p   p

P   P   P

puppet

puppet

Paul is a peppy pig.

Paul is a peppy pig.

Letter Descriptions p: Middle start; slant down under water, up, around, and a tummy. P: Top start; slant down, up, around halfway, and close.

Name _____

Practicing pP

Trace and write.

Pam practiced her part.

Pam practiced her part.

Phillip played a pirate.

Phillip played a pirate.

Peg performed proudly.

Peg performed proudly.

Write the name of a play or show you've seen.

44

Name _____

Review

Write sentences by matching people and their talents by first letters.

Iris	Raj	paints	Will	imitates
recites	Penny	whistles	Jonni	juggles

Write the sentences.
Mona Nor makes magic.

Uma and Yuri yodel.

Name _____

Evaluation

Write the sentences.

Remember: Dot the letters **i** and **j**. Also, leave enough space between words.

Ursula and Rami will send many invitations.

_____

_____

Mom and Junior will come.

_____

_____

Papa, Yogi, and I will serve juice.

_____

_____

✔ **Check Your Handwriting**	Yes	No
Did you dot the letters **i** and **j**?	☐	☐
Did you leave enough space between words?	☐	☐

Name _____

Writing Manuscript qQ and vV

Trace and write.

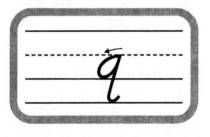 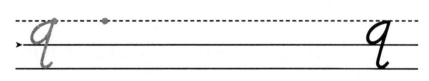

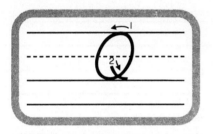 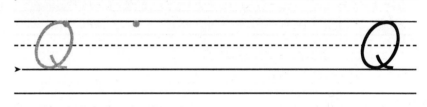

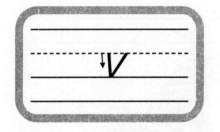

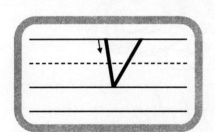

Quin's avocados

Quin's avocados

Letter Descriptions **q:** Middle start; around down, close up, down under water, and a backwards fishhook.
Q: Top start; around down, and close up. Cross with a curve down right. **v:** Middle start; slant down right, and slant up right. **V:** Top start; slant down right, and slant up right.

Practicing Manuscript qQ and vV

Trace and write.

Quentin bought several quarts of milk.

Quentin bought several quarts of milk.

Vivian got vegetables.

Vivian got vegetables.

Write two foods you buy at the grocery store.

Name _____

Writing Manuscript zZ and xX

Trace and write.

$\vec{z}$ z   z

$\vec{Z}$ Z   Z

x   x   x

X   X   X

Zoe's zucchini

Zoe's zucchini

Letter Descriptions z: Middle start; over right, slant down left, and over right. **Z:** Top start; over right, slant down left, and over right. **x:** Middle start; slant down right, and a monkey tail. Cross down left. **X:** Top start; slant down right, and a monkey tail. Cross down left.

Name _____

Practicing Manuscript zZ and xX

Trace and write.

Zelda got a dozen eggs and six frozen pizzas.

Zelda got a dozen eggs and six frozen pizzas.

Xavier needs an extra box of pancake mix.

Xavier needs an extra box of pancake mix.

© Scott Foresman / Addison Wesley

Name _____

Writing Numbers 1 Through 10

Trace and write the numbers.

1

2

3

4

5

6

7

8

9

10

Practicing Numbers 1 Through 10

Trace and write the name, address, and telephone
number of the grocery store.

Good Eats
82439 S. Queens
Zion, IL 60647
(555) 213-1870

Good Eats

82439 S. Queens

Zion, IL 60647

(555) 213-1870

Name _____

Writing Number Words

Trace and write the number words.

one
one

two
two

three
three

four
four

five
five

six
six

seven
seven

eight
eight

nine
nine

ten
ten

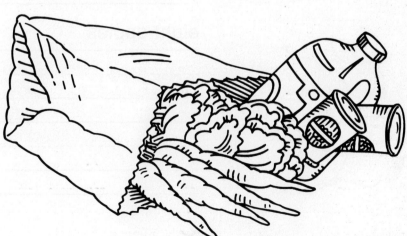

Name _____

Practicing Number Words

Trace and write.

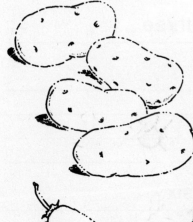

four potatoes

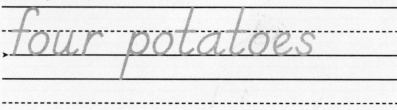

four potatoes

six peppers

six peppers

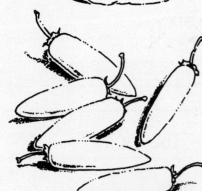

two cakes

two cakes

eight apples

eight apples

54

Name _____

Review

Xavier Vix and Zoe Quay went shopping. Write the children's names, how much they spent, and what they bought.

six
quarts
of juice

Xavier Vix

five
frozen
pizzas

Zoe Quay

Name
_____

Spent
_____

Bought
_____

_____

Name
_____

Spent
_____

Bought
_____

_____

Name _____

Evaluation

Write the sentence.

Remember: Cross the letter **x**. Also, slant all your writing the same way.

Zack Vazquez drove to the excellent Q and X Market.

Write the missing number or number word.

1	*six*
two	7
three	*eight*
four	9
5	10

✓ **Check Your Handwriting**   Yes   No

Did you cross the letter **x**?   ☐   ☐

Did you slant all your writing the same way?   ☐   ☐

56

19

Name _Bayli_   5/4/05

Ready for Cursive

This sign has **manuscript writing.** The letters are not joined together.

> *This way to campgrounds*

This sign has **cursive writing.** The letters are joined together.

> *This way to campgrounds*

Many manuscript and cursive letters look alike. Circle the cursive letters on the sign above that look like manuscript letters.

Read the words in cursive below. Make a ⌣ under the places where the letters are joined. Then write the words in manuscript. The first one is done for you.

campfire

campfire   _campfire_

lantern

lantern   _lantern_

backpack

backpack   _backpack_

© Scott Foresman / Addison Wesley

57

Name _____ *Baya* _____

Strokes That Make Cursive Letters:
Uphill Strokes

To write cursive **l, h, k, t, i, u,** and **e,** add **uphill strokes** to the letters you already know. These letters already have ending strokes. To write cursive **j** and **p,** begin with an uphill stroke and add an ending stroke.

With your finger, trace the uphill stroke in each letter. Circle the ending stroke in each letter.

uphill strokes

l h k t i u e j p

Uphill strokes can be tall or short. Practice each one.

To write a word in cursive, join the ending stroke in one letter to the beginning stroke in the next letter.

The letters **k, i, t,** and **e** begin with uphill strokes. Ending strokes and uphill strokes are joined in the word **kite.** Trace the word.

kite kite

58

Name _Bayli_

Strokes That Make Cursive Letters:
Overhill Strokes

overhill stroke

To write cursive **a, d, c, n, m,** and **x,** add **overhill strokes** to the letters you already know. These letters already have ending strokes. To write cursive **g, y,** and **q,** begin with an overhill stroke and add an ending stroke.

With your finger, trace the overhill stroke in each letter. Circle the ending stroke in each letter.

$$a \quad d \quad c \quad n \quad m \quad x \quad g \quad y \quad q$$

Practice the overhill stroke.

The letters **m, a, n,** and **y** begin with overhill strokes. Ending strokes and overhill strokes are joined in the word **many.** Trace the word.

many   many

many

Name _Bayli_

Strokes That Make Cursive Letters: Sidestrokes

The cursive letters **o, w,** and **b** end with a sidestroke. With your finger trace the sidestroke in each letter.

_o w b_

Practice the sidestroke.

sidestroke

A letter with a sidestroke must join the following letter near the middle line. This changes the beginning stroke of the following letter. Notice how the sidestroke changes **n, y,** and **e** in the words below. Trace the words.

_on_   _by_   _we_

_on_   _by_   _we_

Most cursive letters look like the manuscript letters you already know. The letters **v, z, s, r,** and **f** look different.

Trace the cursive letters. Then circle the uphill letters. Underline the overhill letters. Put a ✔ above the sidestroke letter.

_vv_   _zz_   _ss_   _rr_   _ff_

Name _____ *Bayli* _____

Letter Size and Form

Cursive letters come in the same three sizes as manuscript letters. There are small letters, tall letters, and letters with descenders.

Trace these small letters.

e i

Trace these tall letters.

l t

Trace these letters with descenders.

j q

Here are some things to remember about forming cursive letters.

Some cursive letters must be closed.

o s

Some cursive letters have loops.

k g

You must retrace when you write some cursive letters.

n t

Look at the cursive alphabet below. Trace the letters. Then circle four letters that must be closed. Underline five letters that have loops. Put a ✔ above three letters that have retracing.

a b c d e f g h i j

k l m n o p q r s

t u v w x y z

Name _Bayli_

Letter Slant and Spacing

When you write in cursive, slant all your letters the same way. You may slant your letters to the right or to the left. You may write them straight up and down. Do not slant your letters in different ways.

Which writing is hard to read? Why is it hard?
Which slant do you like? Trace that word.

right   _left_

straight   _different_

Use correct spacing when you write. The letters in a word should be evenly spaced. Leave more space between words than between letters in a word.

Circle the writing that is easier to read. Why is it easier?

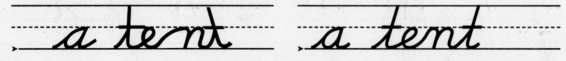

a tent   _a tent_

62

Name _____ *Bayli,*

Writing Cursive l and h

You can see manuscript **l** and **h** in cursive **l** and **h**.
Begin with an uphill stroke. Trace and write the letters.

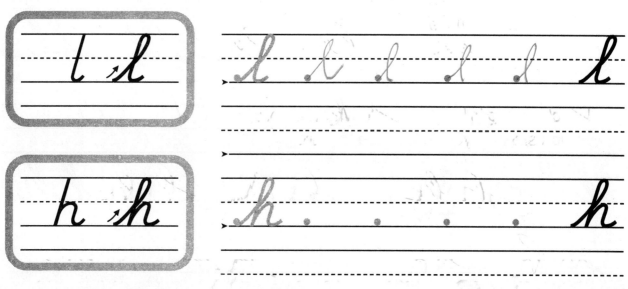

Lila and her family are going camping. Use cursive
to write the first letter of some things they will take.

lantern   hamburger   hammer   lettuce

Letter Descriptions **l:** Uphill high; loop down, and up. **h:** Uphill high; loop down, up over the hill, and up.   63

Name _____

Practicing Cursive l and h

Most cursive letters are joined near the bottom line. Practice joining these letters.

(handwriting practice lines with cursive letters: ll, hh, lh, hl)

Fill in the missing letters. Use cursive.

hill   *hill*

Name _____

Writing Cursive k and t

You can see manuscript **k** and **t** in cursive **k** and **t**.
Begin with an uphill stroke. Trace and write the letters.

Look at what Mr. Kemp took hiking. Use cursive
to write the *last* letter of each thing he took.

l. *t*

2.

3.

4.

5.

l. hat

5. backpack

2. drink

4. flashlight

3. boot

Letter Descriptions k: Uphill high; loop down, up into a little tummy, slant down right, and up. **t:** Uphill high; down, and up. Cross.

Practicing Cursive k and t

Remember that most cursive letters are joined near the bottom line. Trace and write the letters.

th _____ *th*

lk _____ *lk*

ht _____ *ht*

Write the missing letters. Use cursive.

wa__ __

pa__ __

fea__ __ers

ga__ __er

e__ __

lig__ __

elk   light   walk   feathers   path   gather

Writing Cursive i and u

You can see manuscript **i** and **u** in cursive **i** and **u**.
Begin with an uphill stroke. Trace and write the letters.

Remember that most cursive letters are joined near
the bottom line. Practice joining these letters.

Letter Descriptions i: Uphill; down, and up. Add a dot. u: Uphill; down, around, up, down, and up.

Name _____

Practicing Cursive i and u

Trace and write these letters. Remember that most cursive letters are joined near the bottom line.

hu   *hu*

ut   *ut*

li   *li*

ki   *ki*

Now you can join letters in words.
Trace and write the words.

hut   **lit**   **kit**

hut   *lit*   *kit*

Name _____

Writing Cursive e

You can see manuscript **e** in cursive **e**. Begin with an
uphill stroke. Trace and write the letter.

e e   *e . . . . e*

Practice joining these letters.

ee   *ee*

le   *le*

ke   *ke*

el   *el*

Trace and write the words.

hike   **he**

hike   *he*

Letter Description **e**: Uphill; loop down, through, and up.

Practicing Cursive e

Trace and write the words.

tell

tell

like

like

tie

tie

Trace and write the phrases. Remember to leave enough space between words.

the hill hike

the hill hike

the little kettle

the little kettle

Name _____

Writing Cursive j and p

You can see manuscript **j** and **p** in cursive **j** and **p.**
Begin with an uphill stroke. Add an ending stroke.
Trace and write the letters.

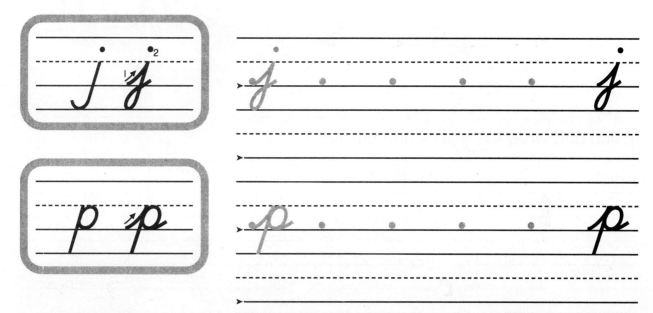

Trace and write the words.

jet

jet

uphill

uphill

keep

keep

Letter Descriptions j: Uphill; down under water, loop up left, and through. Add a dot. **p:** Uphill; down under water, up, around into a tummy, and up.

Name _____

Practicing Cursive j and p

Trace and write the words and phrase.

jeep

jeep

pile

pile

pull

pull

help

help

peek

peek

put

put

the pet pup

the pet pup

Name _____

Review

Use the words and pictures to answer the riddles.

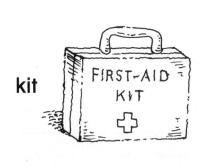 kit

 kettle

 pup

jeep

heel

hill

1. I'm good to have when someone gets hurt.

> _____

2. You can cook soup in me.

> _____

3. I am good for sledding in the winter and hiking in the summer.

> _____

4. I follow your toes on every walk.

> _____

5. I want to be your best friend.

> _____

6. I need four wheels to make me go.

> _____

Name _____

Evaluation

Remember: Dot the letters **i** and **j**. Also, leave enough space between words.

Write the phrases.

kept the jeep

➤ _____

the little pup

➤ _____

the hike up the hill

➤ _____

the help kit

➤ _____

✓ **Check Your Handwriting**   Yes   No
  Did you dot the letters **i** and **j**?   ☐   ☐
  Did you leave enough space between words?   ☐   ☐

Name _____

Writing Cursive a

You can see manuscript **a** in cursive **a**. Begin with
an overhill stroke. Trace and write the letter.

a a   *a* · · · · *a*

Practice joining these letters.

ai   *ai*

al   *al*

Trace and write the words.

alike

alike

tail

tail

Letter Description a: Overhill; back, around down, close up, down, and up.

Name _____

Practicing Cursive a

Trace and write the words.

ape

ape

apple

apple

eat

eat

Trace and write the phrases. Remember that most cursive letters are joined near the bottom line.

at a plate

at a plate

ate that apple

ate that apple

Name _____

Writing Cursive d and c

You can see manuscript **d** and **c** in cursive **d** and **c**.
Begin with an overhill stroke. Trace and write the letters.

 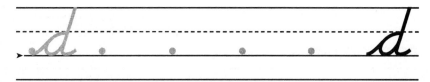

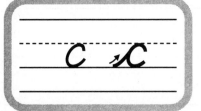 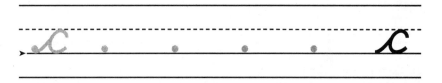

Trace and write these words.

dad

child

ahead

Letter Descriptions **d**: Overhill; back, around down, touch, up high, down, and up. **c**: Overhill; back, around, down, and up.

77

Name _____

Practicing Cursive d and c

Trace and write the phrases.

held the chick

held the chick

a lettuce diet

a lettuce diet

pecked at each piece

pecked at each piece

a cute duck

a cute duck

Writing Cursive n and m

You can see manuscript **n** and **m** in cursive **n** and **m**.
Begin with an overhill stroke. Trace and write the letters.

n ;*m*　　　*m* .　　.　　.　　*m*

m ;*m*　　　*m* .　　.　　*m*

Trace and write the words.

mealtime

mealtime

nap

nap

Letter Descriptions n: Overhill; down, up over the hill, and up.　m: Overhill; down, up over the hill, up over the hill again, and up.

Practicing Cursive n and m

Trace and write the phrases.

an animal

an animal

a mama elephant

a mama elephant

a plump llama and a thin camel

a plump llama

and a thin camel

Name _____

Writing Cursive g and x

You can see manuscript **g** and **x** in cursive **g** and **x**.
Begin with an overhill stroke. Add an ending stroke
to **g**. Trace and write the letters.

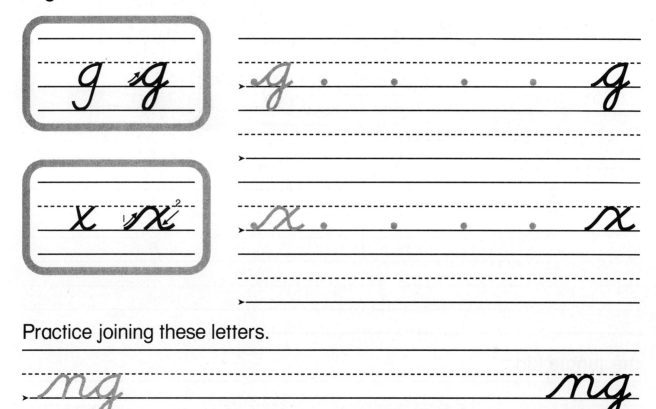

Practice joining these letters.

Trace and write the word.

exiting

Letter Descriptions g: Overhill; back, around down, close up, down under water, loop up left, and through.
x: Overhill; slant down right, and up. Cross down left.

81

Practicing Cursive g and x

Trace and write the phrases.

examine a lung

examine a lung

the jungle king

the jungle king

a gentle exam

a gentle exam

Writing Cursive y and q

You can see manuscript **y** and **q** in cursive **y** and **q**.
Begin with an overhill stroke. Add an ending stroke.
Trace and write the letters.

y y   *y .   .   .   .   y*

q q   *q .   .   .   .   q*

Trace and write the words.

many   **quickly**

many   *quickly*

Letter Descriptions y: Overhill; down, around, up, down under water, loop up left, and through. **q:** Overhill; back, around down, close up, down under water, loop up right, touch, and up.

Practicing Cursive y and q

Trace and write the word and phrases.

yummy

yummy

quite tiny

quite tiny

play quietly

play quietly

yank and yelp

yank and yelp

Review

Write the words and phrases in the
box that will complete the story.

cackling chicken	many exciting animals
quacking duck	quiet quail
napping panda	cuddly

Today at the zoo, I saw ____ ____
____. When I went to the farm
area, I saw a ____ ____ and a ____
____. At the bears' area, I saw a
____ ____. He looked so ____. At
the birds' area, I saw a ____ ____.

Name _____

Evaluation

Remember: The letters **g**, **y**, and **q** have descenders that touch the line below. Also, most letters join at the bottom line.

Write the phrases.

a huge mane

_____

> _____

a quacking duck

_____

> _____

an excellent lunch

_____

> _____

my exciting day

_____

> _____

✔ **Check Your Handwriting**   Yes   No

Do your descenders touch the line below?   ☐   ☐

Did you join letters at the bottom line?   ☐   ☐

Name _____

Writing Cursive o and w

You can see manuscript **o** and **w** in cursive **o** and **w**. Begin cursive **o** with an overhill stroke. Begin cursive **w** with an uphill stroke. Both letters end with a sidestroke. Trace and write the letters.

o   o   *o   .   .   .   .   o*

w   w   *w   .   .   .   .   w*

Cursive **o** and **w** join the next letter near the middle line. This changes the beginning stroke of the next letter. Trace and write the words.

ocean   **waddle**

ocean   *waddle*

Letter Descriptions **o:** Overhill; back, around down, close up, and sidestroke. **w:** Uphill; down, around, up, down, around, up again, and sidestroke.

Name _____

Practicing Cursive o and w

Trace and write the phrases.

a cool, windy day

a cool, windy day

walking along the ocean at noon

walking along the

ocean at noon

watching a whale

watching a whale

Writing Cursive b

Cursive **b** looks a little like manuscript **b**.
Begin with an uphill stroke and end with a
sidestroke. Trace and write the letter.

b b b . . . . . b

Cursive **b** joins the next letter near the middle
line. This changes the beginning stroke of the
next letter. Trace and write the words.

boat

boat

bait

bait

balance

balance

below

below

Letter Description **b**: Uphill high; loop down, around, up, and sidestroke.

Name _____

Practicing Cursive b

Trace and write the phrases.

a boy with a book

a boy with a book

a black beach ball

a black beach ball

a big blue bucket

a big blue bucket

a boat by the beach

a boat by the beach

Writing Cursive v and z

Cursive **v** and **z** do not look like manuscript **v** and **z**.
Begin cursive **v** and **z** with an overhill stroke. Cursive
v ends with a sidestroke. Trace and write the letters.

Trace and write the words.

vacation

vacation

lazy

lazy

doze

doze

vine

vine

Letter Descriptions v: Overhill; down, around, up, and sidestroke. z: Overhill; around down, around again, and down under water, loop up left, and through.

Name _____

Practicing Cursive v and z

Trace and write the phrases.

a dazzling view

a dazzling view

gazing at a village in a valley

gazing at a village
in a valley

a lovely evening

a lovely evening

Name _____

Writing Cursive s

Cursive **s** does not look like manuscript **s**. Begin cursive
s with an uphill stroke. Trace and write the letter.

S   s   s   .   .   .   .   s

Trace and write the words.

sea

sea

sand

sand

sun

sun

sailboats

sailboats

seashells

seashells

seashore

seashore

seaweed

seaweed

Letter Description **s**: Uphill; down, around, close, and up.

Practicing Cursive s

Trace and write the phrases.

a sunset swim

a sunset swim

some small waves

some small waves

splashes and swims in the sea

splashes and swims in the sea

Writing Cursive r

Cursive **r** does not look like manuscript **r**. Begin cursive **r** with an uphill stroke. Trace and write the letter.

r r   *r · · · · r*

Trace and write the words.

parrot

parrot

large

large

pretty

pretty

bird

bird

colors

colors

Letter Description r: Uphill; sidestroke, down, and up.

Name _____

Practicing Cursive r

Trace and write the phrases.

under the water

under the water

a pretty coral reef

a pretty coral reef

crabs near a diver

crabs near a diver

a very large rock

a very large rock

Name _____

Writing Cursive f

Cursive **f** does not look like manuscript **f**. Begin cursive **f** with an uphill stroke. Trace and write the letter.

Trace and write the words.

friendly

fish

float

film

Practicing Cursive f

Trace and write the phrases.

floppy flippers

floppy flippers

fast flying fish

fast flying fish

four fat funny fish finding food

four fat funny fish
finding food

Name _____

Review

Use the phrases in the box to
complete each pair of sentences.

┌─────────────────────────────┐
│ like a fish out of water   │
│ as red as a lobster   │
└─────────────────────────────┘

Bev had a bad sunburn. She was

_____

_____ •

Ken was the only boy at his sister's party. He felt

_____

_____

_____

_____ •

Use the words in the box that begin with the same
letter to write a tongue twister.

┌──┐
│ only   below   dazzling   deep   very   │
│ divers   down   fish   swimming   diving   │
└──┘

_____

_____

_____

_____

Name _____

Evaluation

Remember: Sidestroke letters **o, w,** and **b** each join the next letter near the middle line. Also, small letters should touch the middle line.

Write the phrases.

dives under water

gazes at seaweed and lovely starfish

big fish zooming by

a fun adventure

✓ **Check Your Handwriting**   Yes   No

Do each of your sidestroke letters join
the next letter near the middle line?   ☐   ☐

Do your small letters touch the middle line?   ☐   ☐

Name _____

Letter Size and Form

All capital cursive letters touch the top and bottom lines.
Some capital letters also have descenders that touch the
line below. Be sure to form your letters correctly.

Some capital letters are closed.

Some capital letters have loops.

You must retrace when you write
some capital letters. That means
you go over a line you've written.

Some capital letters have
descenders. The descenders
should touch the line below.

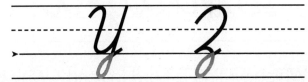

Trace the capital letters below. Then circle four letters
that must be closed. Underline five letters that have
loops. Put a ✔ above two letters that have descenders.
Put a box around four letters that have retracing.

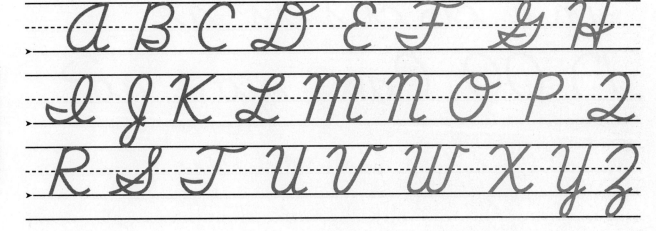

Letter Slant

Slant capital letters in the same direction as lower-case letters. You may slant letters to the right or to the left. You may write them straight up and down.

Right   *Left*

Straight   *Different*

Which writing is hard to read? Why is it hard?

Numbers and punctuation marks should slant in the same direction as letters. Leave more space between sentences than between words. Look at these sentences written two ways. Trace the sentences written correctly.

The circus is at 12:00. Can you go?

The circus is at 12:00. Can you go?

Name _____

Writing Cursive A and C

Cursive **A** does not look like manuscript **A**. Cursive **C** looks like manuscript **C**. Trace and write the letters.

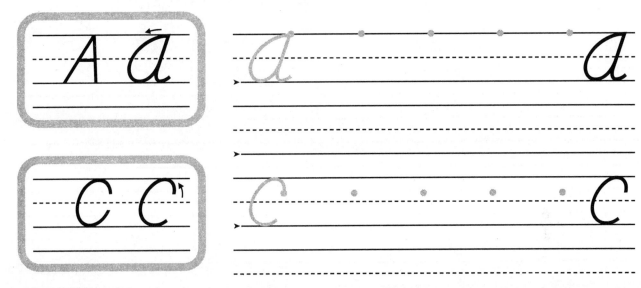

Trace and write the sentence. Be sure to join cursive **A** and **C** to the letter that comes next.

Come to the great Apollo Circus!

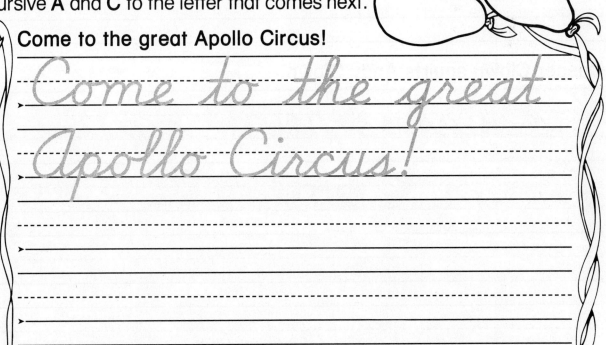

Letter Descriptions   A: Top start; around down, close up, down, and up.   **C:** Start below the top; curve up, around, down, and up.

Name _____

Practicing Cursive A and C

Trace and write the sentences.

Circus time is here!

Circus time is here!

Artie Acrobat swings.

Artie Acrobat swings.

Casper Clown squirts Andy Clown.

Casper Clown squirts Andy Clown.

Writing Cursive E and O

Cursive **E** looks a little like manuscript **E**. You can see manuscript **O** in cursive **O**. Trace and write the letters.

E $\mathcal{E}$

O O

Trace and write the sentences. Join **E** to the letter that follows it, but do not join **O**.

Emma dances.

Emma dances.

Oats prances.

Oats prances.

Letter Descriptions **E:** Start below the top; curve up, around to the middle, around again to the bottom line, and up. **O:** Top start; around down, close up, loop right, through, and stop.

Name _____

Practicing Cursive E and O

Trace and write the sentences.

One circus was here.

One circus was here.

> _____

Orbit Circus goes to Europe in October.

Orbit Circus goes to

Europe in October.

> _____

> _____

Every circus is fun!

Every circus is fun!

> _____

Name _____

Review

Choose names from the box for each circus act.
Write the names under the pictures.

| Electric Eva | Olga Owl | Coco Clown | Ajax Acrobat |

Name _____

Evaluation

Remember: A, C, and **E** should join the letters that follow. Also, capitals should touch the top and bottom lines.

Write the sentences.

Emo Elephant enters.

Coco the clown went to Clown College.

Aki loves the circus.

✓ **Check Your Handwriting**

Do the capital letters **A, C,** and **E** join the letters that follow them?

Do all your capital letters touch the top and bottom lines?

Yes   No

☐   ☐

☐   ☐

Writing Cursive H and K

You can see manuscript **H** and **K** in cursive **H** and **K**. Trace and write the letters.

Trace and write the sentence. Join **K** to the letter that follows it. Do not join **H** to the next letter.

Kathy Hobbs works at Kane Hospital.

Kathy Hobbs works at Kane Hospital.

Letter Descriptions H: Start below the top; make a cane. Top start, to the right; down, up, left, touch, loop right, through, and stop. **K:** Start below the top; make a cane. Top start, to the right; slant down left, touch, slant down right, and up.

Practicing Cursive H and K

Trace and write the sentences.

Hal King is a nurse at Kare Hospital.

Hal King is a nurse at Kare Hospital.

He says, "Hello. How do you feel today?"

He says, "Hello. How do you feel today?"

Name _____

Writing Cursive N and M

Cursive **N** and **M** look a little like manuscript
N and **M**. Trace and write the letters.

$\mathcal{N}$ $\mathcal{n}$

$\mathcal{n}$ $\cdot$ $\cdot$ $\cdot$ $\cdot$ $\mathcal{n}$

$\mathcal{M}$ $\mathcal{m}$

$\mathcal{m}$ $\cdot$ $\cdot$ $\cdot$ $\cdot$ $\mathcal{m}$

Trace and write the sentence. Join cursive
N and **M** to the letters that follow them.

Mr. Nash plays with the Melody Makers.

Mr. Nash plays with
the Melody Makers.

Letter Descriptions N: Start below the top; make a cane, up over the hill, and up. **M:** Start below the top;
make a cane, up over the hill, up over the hill again, and up.

Name _____

Practicing Cursive N and M

Trace and write the sentences.

Meet the Music Notes.

Meet the Music Notes.

Nora Moreno drums.

Nora Moreno drums.

Nina Miki strums.

Nina Miki strums.

Marsha North hums.

Marsha North hums.

Writing Cursive U and V

Cursive **U** looks very much like manuscript **U**.
Cursive **V** looks a little like manuscript **V**.
Trace and write the letters.

Trace and write the sentence. Join cursive **U** to
the letter that follows it. Do not join cursive **V**.

Uncle Vic is a waiter at the Village Cafe.

Uncle Vic is a waiter
at the Village Cafe.

Letter Descriptions U: Start below the top; make a cane, around, up, down, and up. **V:** Start below the top; make a cane, around, slant up right, sidestroke, and stop.

Name _____

Practicing Cursive U and V

Trace and write the sentences.

Visit Vi's Vegetarian Cafe in Union, Utah.

Visit Vi's Vegetarian

Cafe in Union, Utah.

Ugo Venton hosts.

Ugo Venton hosts.

Velma Ulrich cooks.

Velma Ulrich cooks.

114

Writing Cursive Y and W

Cursive **Y** and **W** look a little like manuscript
Y and **W**. Trace and write the letters.

Y y

W w

Trace and write the sentence. Join
Y to the next letter. Do not join **W**.

Wesley Yager works for Wick Airlines.

*Wesley Yager works
for Wick Airlines.*

Letter Descriptions Y: Start below the top; make a cane, up, around, down under water, loop up left, and through. **W:** Start below the top; make a cane, around, up, down, around, up again, sidestroke, and stop.

Name _____

Practicing Cursive Y and W

Trace and write the sentences.

Will York is a pilot.

Will York is a pilot.

Yoko Wada is a copilot for Wing Air.

Yoko Wada is a copilot for Wing Air.

Welcome aboard!

Welcome aboard!

Name _____

Review

What is each person's job? Read what each
person has to say. Then answer the questions.

Who is the artist?

_____

Who is the dentist?

_____

Who is the teacher?

_____

Who is the veterinarian?

_____

Name _____

Evaluation

Write the sentences.

Remember: The descender on the letter **Y** should touch the line below. Also, slant all of your writing the same way.

Kevin Ubert reports for <u>Weekly News</u>.

He interviewed Mayor Yolanda Vega.

What an interview it was!

✓ **Check Your Handwriting**　　　　　　**Yes**　　**No**

Does the descender on the letter **Y** touch
the line below?　　　　　　　　　　□　　□

Does all your writing slant the same way?　□　　□

Name _____

Writing Cursive T and F

Cursive **T** and **F** look a little like manuscript
T and **F**. Trace and write the letters.

Trace and write the sentence. Do not join
T and **F** to the letters that follow them.

Fred Tate will be eight on Tuesday.

Letter Descriptions T: Start below the top; down, around, up, and sidestroke. Wavy cross. **F:** Start below the top; down, around, up, and sidestroke. Wavy cross and a straight cross.

Name _____

Practicing Cursive T and F

Trace and write the sentences.

Today is Terri Frankel's birthday.

Today is Terri

Frankel's birthday.

The party's Friday.

The party's Friday.

Tim Feng can't go.

Tim Feng can't go.

Writing Cursive B

Cursive **B** looks like manuscript **B**.
Trace and write the letter.

Trace and write the sentences. Do not
join cursive **B** to the letter that follows it.

Birthdays are fun.

Birthdays are fun.

Blow out candles.

Blow out candles.

Bite into the cake.

Bite into the cake.

Letter Description B: Top start; down, up, around halfway, around again, touch, sidestroke, and stop.

Name _____

Practicing Cursive B

Trace and write the sentences.

Bring a present for Bev Bell's birthday.

Bring a present for

Bev Bell's birthday.

Ben will give Bev the book Button Box.

Ben will give Bev

the book Button Box.

Writing Cursive P and R

You can see manuscript **P** and **R** in cursive
P and **R**. Trace and write the letters.

$\mathcal{P}$ $\mathcal{P}$ $\mathcal{P}$ $\mathcal{P}$

$\mathcal{R}$ $\mathcal{R}$ $\mathcal{R}$ $\mathcal{R}$

Trace and write the sentence. Join **R**
to the next letter. Do not join **P**.

Remind Ruth about Phil's party.

Remind Ruth about

Phil's party.

Letter Descriptions P: Top start; down, up, around halfway, and close. **R:** Top start; down, up, around
halfway, close, slant down right, and up.

Practicing Cursive P and R

Trace and write the sentences.

Please wrap Paula's present, Richard.

Please wrap Paula's

present, Richard.

Ribbon is here.

Ribbon is here.

Pick paper, Renee.

Pick paper, Renee.

Name _____

Review

It's Roxanna's birthday. She's going to have a party.
Use the information in the balloons to fill out the invitation.

Roxanna Prado

32 Tower Trail

Birthday Party

Friday, February 21

You're Invited!

What: _____
_____
_____

For Whom: _____
_____

When: _____
_____

Where: _____
_____

Name _____

Evaluation

Remember: Do not join **T, F, B,** or **P** to the next letter. Also, close the letters **B, P,** and **R.**

Write the sentences.

Fay and Bret Rose surprised their papa.

_____

> _____

_____

> _____

_____

They gave him a birthday party.

_____

> _____

_____

> _____

_____

"Thanks," Papa said.

_____

> _____

_____

✓ **Check Your Handwriting**   **Yes**   **No**

Did you remember not to join **T, F, B,** or
P to the next letter?   ☐   ☐

Did you close **B, P,** and **R?**   ☐   ☐

Writing Cursive G and S

Cursive **G** and **S** do not look like manuscript
G and **S**. Trace and write the letters.

G G

S S

Trace and write the sentence. Do not join cursive
G and **S** to the letters that follow them.

Gina Gray went to Statue Showroom.

Gina Gray went to Statue Showroom.

Letter Descriptions G: Bottom start; uphill high, loop through the middle, up, curve down, around, through the uphill, sidestroke, and stop. **S:** Bottom start; uphill high, loop through the middle, curve down, around, through the uphill, sidestroke, and stop.

127

Name _____

Practicing Cursive G and S

Trace and write the sentences.

Go to Gil's Gallery.

Go to Gil's Gallery.

See <u>Green Smoke</u>.

See Green Smoke.

Sid saw the statue.

Sid saw the statue.

"Great!" Sid said.

"Great!" Sid said.

Name _____

Writing Cursive I

Cursive **I** does not look like manuscript **I**.
Trace and write the letter.

Trace and write the sentences. Join cursive
I to the letter that follows it. Always write
the pronoun **I** with a capital letter.

Inez and I went to Insect Institute.

I like insects.

Name _____

Practicing Cursive I

Trace and write the sentences.

Ira wants to see "Incredible Insects."

Ira wants to see

"Incredible Insects."

"I'll go," I said.

"I'll go," I said.

"Invite Isabel too."

"Invite Isabel too."

Name _____

Writing Cursive Z and Q

Cursive **Z** and **Q** do not look like manuscript
Z and **Q**. Trace and write the letters.

Trace and write the sentence. Join cursive
Z and **Q** to the letters that follow them.

"Zoos are interesting places," Quincy says.

© Scott Foresman / Addison Wesley

Letter Descriptions **Z:** Start below the top; curve up, around, down, around again, and down under water, loop up left, and through. **Q:** Start below the top; curve up, around, down, loop right, and up.

Name _____

Practicing Cursive Z and Q

Trace and write the sentences.

Zelda Quintos went to the Quebec Zoo.

Zelda Quintos went

to the Quebec Zoo.

Zebras grazed lazily.

Zebras grazed lazily.

Quails squawked.

Quails squawked.

132

Name _____

Writing Cursive D

Cursive **D** looks something like manuscript
D. Trace and write the letter.

$\mathcal{D}$ $\mathcal{D}$ $\mathcal{D}$ $\mathcal{D}$ $\mathcal{D}$ $\mathcal{D}$

Trace and write the sentences. Do not
join cursive **D** to the next letter.

Don't miss the Dinosaur Museum!

Don't miss the

Dinosaur Museum!

Dee says it's great.

Dee says it's great.

Letter Description **D**: Top start; down, loop right, curve up, around, close, loop right, through, and stop.

Practicing Cursive D

Trace and write the sentences.

Dean Diaz went to the Dallas Museum.

Dean Diaz went to

the Dallas Museum.

Dave Dill went too.

Dave Dill went too.

Did Dr. Dan and Dad see an exhibit?

Did Dr. Dan and

Dad see an exhibit?

Writing Cursive J

Cursive **J** does not look like manuscript **J**.
Trace and write the letter.

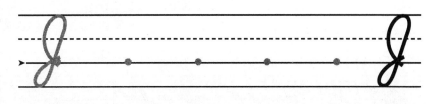

Trace and write the sentences. Join
cursive **J** to the letter that follows it.
Julie studies planets.

Julie studies planets.

Jon looks at stars.

Jon looks at stars.

Letter Description J: Bottom start; curve up, around, touch on the way down under water, loop up left, and through.

Practicing Cursive J

Trace and write the sentences.

Journey to Jupiter!

Journey to Jupiter!

Jump into a rocket!

Jump into a rocket!

Join us at the Juno Joy Planetarium.

Join us at the Juno Joy Planetarium.

Name _____

Writing Cursive X and L

You can see manuscript **X** in cursive **X**. Cursive **L** looks
something like manuscript **L**. Trace and write the letters.

Trace and write the sentence. Join cursive
L to the letter that follows it. Do not join
cursive **X** to the next letter.

Let's go to Xavier's Music Museum.

Letter Descriptions X: Start below the top; curve up, slant down right, and up. Cross down left. **L:** Start below
the top; uphill, loop down, loop right, and up.

Name _____

Practicing Cursive X and L

Trace and write the sentences.

Xylophones are in Room X, Lisa.

Xylophones are in

Room X, Lisa.

Look at these, Lou.

Look at these, Lou.

Listen to this, Lori.

Listen to this, Lori.

Name _____

Review

Write answers to the questions.

The Jazz Studio opens in December.

Zach

Xylophones will be there. Let's go.

Gina

It will be fun.

Quin

Who is talking?

_____ | _____ | _____

What did the first child say?

What did the second child say?

What did the third child say?

Name _____

Evaluation

Write the words on the museum signs.

Remember: The descenders on the letters **Z** and **J** should touch the lines below. Also, all your letters should be the correct size.

Gems and Jewels

Zuni Indian Life

Stars and Quasars

X-ray Display

✓ **Check Your Handwriting**   Yes   No

Do the descenders on the letters **Z** and **J**
touch the lines below?   ☐   ☐

Are your letters the correct size?   ☐   ☐

Index

Adjusting writing to space, 32, 33, 34

Capitalization
  abbreviations, 111, 134
  names, places, and things
    (*See* Proper nouns.)
  pronoun *I,* 36, 129, 130
  titles, 118, 122, 128

Critical thinking, 18, 23, 28, 44, 55, 73, 85, 107, 117, 139

Cross-curricular connections
  fine arts, 35, 36, 37, 38, 42, 43, 44
  health and safety, 29, 30, 31, 32
  language arts, 20, 42, 45, 63, 64, 65, 66, 85, 99
  mathematics, 50, 51, 53, 54, 55, 56
  science, 135, 136
  social studies, 109, 110, 111, 112, 113, 114, 115, 116, 117, 118, 127, 128, 129, 131, 132, 133, 134, 135, 136, 137, 139, 140

Descenders, 5, 12, 61, 86, 101, 118, 140

Evaluation of handwriting, 6–7, 24, 34, 46, 56, 74, 86, 100, 108, 118, 126, 140

Legibility
  adjusting writing to space, 32, 33, 34
  letter and word spacing, 7, 14, 46, 62, 70, 74
  letter size and form, 6, 12, 61, 101, 108, 126, 140
  letter slant, 7, 13, 24, 56, 62, 102, 118
  sentence spacing, 102

Letter and word spacing, 7, 14, 46, 62, 70, 74

Letter descriptions, 8–11

Letter size and form, 6, 12, 61, 101, 108, 126, 140

Letter slant, 7, 13, 24, 56, 62, 102, 118

Letters
  cursive capitals
    A, 103–104; **B,** 121–122;
    C, 103–104; **D,** 133–134;
    E, 105–106; **F,** 119–120;
    G, 127–128; **H,** 109–110;
    I, 129–130; **J,** 135–136;
    K, 109–110; **L,** 137–138;
    M, 111–112; **N,** 111–112;
    O, 105–106; **P,** 123–124;
    Q, 131–132; **R,** 123–124;
    S, 127–128; **T,** 119–120;
    U, 113–114; **V,** 113–114;
    W, 115–116; **X,** 137–138;
    Y, 115–116; **Z,** 131–132
  cursive lower-case
    a, 75–76; **b,** 89–90;
    c, 77–78; **d,** 77–78;
    e, 69–70; **f,** 97–98;
    g, 81–82; **h,** 63–64;
    i, 67–68; **j,** 71–72;
    k, 65–66; **l,** 63–64;
    m, 79–80; **n,** 79–80;
    o, 87–88; **p,** 71–72;
    q, 83–84; **r,** 95–96;
    s, 93–94; **t,** 65–66;
    u, 67–68; **v,** 91–92;
    w, 87–88; **x,** 81–82;
    y, 83–84; **z,** 91–92
  manuscript
    aA, 15–16; **bB,** 27–28;
    cC, 19–20; **dD,** 17–18;
    eE, 21–22; **fF,** 25–26;
    gG, 19–20; **hH,** 29–30;
    iI, 35–36; **jJ,** 39–40;
    kK, 31–32; **lL,** 27–28;
    mM, 41–42; **nN,** 41–42;
    oO, 17–18; **pP,** 43–44;
    qQ, 47–48; **rR,** 39–40;
    sS, 21–22; **tT,** 29–30;
    uU, 35–36; **vV,** 47–48;
    wW, 37–38; **xX,** 49–50;
    yY, 37–38; **zZ,** 49–50

Number descriptions, 9

Numbers, 51–52, 55, 56, 102, 125

Number words, 18, 25, 50, 53–54, 55, 56, 98, 119

Proper nouns, 15, 16, 17, 18, 19, 20, 21, 22, 23, 24, 25, 26, 27, 28, 29, 30, 31, 33, 34, 35, 37, 38, 39, 40, 41, 42, 43, 44, 45, 46, 47, 48, 49, 50, 52, 55, 56, 103, 104, 105, 106, 107, 108, 109, 110, 111, 112, 113, 114, 115, 116, 117, 118, 119, 120, 122, 123, 124, 125, 126, 127, 128, 129, 130, 131, 132, 133, 134, 135, 136, 137, 138, 139, 140

Punctuation practice
  apostrophe, 15, 16, 18, 21, 29, 34, 36, 42, 47, 49, 114, 120, 122, 123, 124, 128, 133, 137, 139
  colon, 102
  comma, 30, 34, 38, 46, 52, 88, 110, 114, 124, 125, 126, 130, 131, 138
  dollars and cents, 55
  exclamation mark, 34, 36, 38, 103, 104, 106, 116, 118, 128, 133, 136
  hyphen, 34, 52
  parentheses, 52
  period, 14, 16, 18, 20, 22, 24, 26, 28, 30, 32, 34, 36, 38, 40, 42, 43, 44, 45, 46, 48, 50, 52, 55, 56, 102, 104, 105, 106, 108, 109, 110, 111, 112, 113, 114, 115, 116, 118, 119, 120, 121, 122, 123, 124, 126, 127, 128, 129, 130, 131, 132, 133, 134, 135, 136, 137, 138, 139
  question mark, 13, 14, 24, 30, 102, 110, 134
  quotation marks, 110, 126, 128, 130, 131
  underline, 118, 122, 128

Review of handwriting, 23, 33, 45, 55, 73, 85, 99, 107, 117, 125, 139

Sentence spacing, 102

Strokes that make cursive letters

ending, 58, 59, 71, 81, 83

joining, 57–60, 64, 66, 67, 68, 69, 76, 86, 87, 89, 100, 103, 105, 108, 109, 111, 113, 115, 119, 121, 123, 126, 127, 129, 131, 133, 135, 137

overhill, 59, 75, 77, 79, 81, 83, 87, 91

sidestroke, 60, 87, 89, 91, 100

uphill, 58, 63, 65, 67, 69, 71, 87, 89, 93, 95, 97

Themes

Animals, 15–24

At the circus, 103–108

At the zoo, 75–86

Bicycles, 25–34

Birthdays, 119–126

Camping, 63–74

Grocery shopping, 47–56

Jobs, 109–118

Places to visit, 127–140

Plays and shows, 35–46

Vacations, 87–100

Transition to cursive, 57–62

Writing, functional/everyday

address, 52, 125

captions, 107

classifying, 18, 44

creative, 16, 40

invitation, 125

labels, 33

riddles, 73

signs, 34, 140

similes, 99

tongue twister, 99

unscramble a sentence, 20, 42

Writing posture, 4